Oh, the doors you will open!

HARCOURT SCHOOL PUBLISHERS

STORYtown

Spring Forward

Senior Authors
Isabel L. Beck • Roger C. Farr • Dorothy S. Strickland

Authors
Alma Flor Ada • Roxanne F. Hudson • Margaret G. McKeown
Robin C. Scarcella • Julie A. Washington

Consultants
F. Isabel Campoy • Tyrone C. Howard • David A. Monti

Harcourt
SCHOOL PUBLISHERS

www.harcourtschool.com

Spring Forward

SCHOOL PUBLISHERS

www.harcourtschool.com

Theme 1
Follow Me

Contents

Social Studies

Social Studies

Theme ② One for All

Social Studies

Social Studies

Paired Selections

Themes 1 and 2 Big Books

The Lost Dog

Decodable Books 1–6

Comprehension Strategies

Before You Read

Look at the pictures. Think about what you already know.

Set a purpose.

I want to find out about frogs.

While You Read

Ask questions.

What do frogs eat?

Reread.

I'll read this page again.

Answer questions.

Oh! Some frogs eat bugs.

Read

This is like another book I read. I learned about how butterflies change.

low Me

▶ *Untitled*, Maja Anderson

Contents

Lesson 1

1 Get Started **Story**

Tag

by Nancy Furstinger
Photographs by Steve Williams

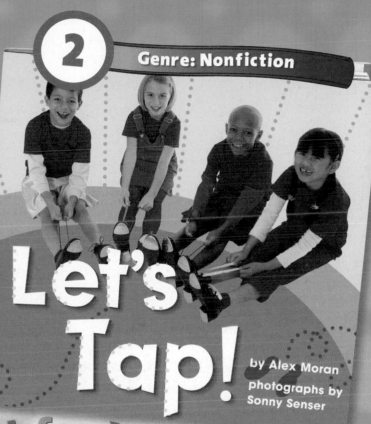

2 Genre: Nonfiction

Let's Tap!

by Alex Moran
photographs by
Sonny Senser

Good for You!
Toddler Rhymes for Toddler Times

original rhymes by
Stephanie Calmenson

pictures by
Melissa Sweet

3 Genre: Poetry

Phonics
Words with short vowel <u>a</u>

Words to Know

Review

who

Tag

by Nancy Furstinger
photographs by
Steve Williams

16

Sam ran.

Sam can tag.

Dan can tag.

Pam can tag.

Pat can tag.

Who can tag Dad?

Sam can!

Focus Skill

 ## Make Predictions

When we read, we think about what might happen next. We **make predictions**.

Look at the pictures.

You can predict that the children will probably get on their bikes and ride away.

Look at these pictures. Tell what might happen next. Why do you think so?

Try This!

Look at the pictures. Tell what you think will happen next.

GO online   www.harcourtschool.com/storytown

Words to Know

High-Frequency Words

let's

help

now

Let's tap.

I can **help** you.

Now you can do it!

 www.harcourtschool.com/storytown

Let's Tap!
by Alex Moran
photographs by
Sonny Senser

Nonfiction

Genre Study

In **nonfiction**, the pictures and words work together to give information.

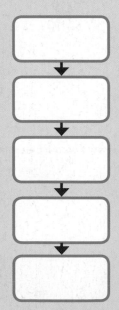

Comprehension Strategy

Answer Questions

Answering questions as you read will help you think about what is happening.

28

Let's Tap!

by Alex Moran   photographs by Sonny Senser

I can tap.

Can you tap?

I can help you.

Tap, tap.

We can tap.

Can you tap?

We can help you.

Tap, tap.

Now let's tap!

Think Critically

1 Do you think the children will help others learn to tap? Why do you think that? MAKE PREDICTIONS

2 How many children are tapping together at the end? NOTE DETAILS

3 Do the children like to tap dance? How can you tell? DRAW CONCLUSIONS

4 How do the children learn the tap dance? MAKE INFERENCES

5 **WRITE** What would you like to learn how to do? Write about it.

WRITING RESPONSE

Meet the Photographer
Sonny Senser

Sonny Senser enjoys taking pictures, because pictures keep memories of his friends and family forever. Sonny enjoyed photographing this story. He says that it reminds him of how his niece and nephew love to dance in the living room when his family gets together.

 www.harcourtschool.com/storytown

Wag, Hop, Hide!

by Stephanie Calmenson

Puppies wag.
Bunnies hop.
Kittens pounce.
Don't stop!

42

Birds flap.
Bugs crawl.
Turtles hide.
We do it all!

Connections

Comparing Texts

1 Tell what you like about the story and the poem. How are they alike? How are they different?

2 Tell what kind of dance or movement you would like to try.

3 If you made up your own kind of dance, what would you call it? What would it look like?

Writing

Think about a time when you were in a performance. What did you do? Write a sentence about it.

I was in a show at school.

Phonics

Make and read new words.

Start with **pat**.

Change | t | to | n |.

Change | p | to | r |.

Change | n | to | g |.

Change | r | to | t |.

Fluency Practice

Practice reading "Let's Tap!" aloud with a friend. Read one page until you can read all of the words correctly. Then listen to your friend read. Continue reading until you can read the story smoothly.

Reading-Writing Connection

Sentences About Us

"Let's Tap!" is about boys and girls who like to dance. We read the story. Then we wrote about what we like to do.

- ▶ **First, we talked about the story.**

- ▶ **Then, we named things we like to do.**

► **Last, we read our sentences.**

Student Writing Model

Zack likes to sing.

Hayley likes to play soccer.

Liz likes to read.

Beto likes to draw.

Contents

Lesson 2

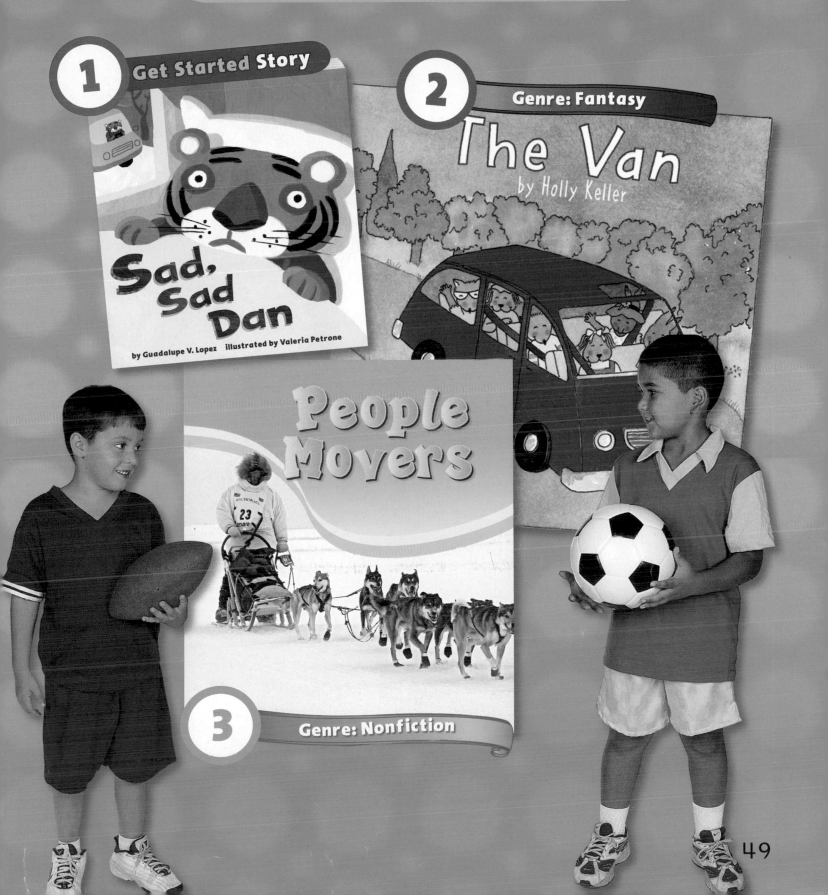

1 Get Started Story

Sad, Sad Dan

by Guadalupe V. Lopez illustrated by Valeria Petrone

2 Genre: Fantasy

The Van

by Holly Keller

People Movers

3 Genre: Nonfiction

Sad, Sad Dan

by Guadalupe V. Lopez

illustrated by Valeria Petrone

I am Dan.

I am a sad, sad cat.

Look at Pam.

Pam has bags.

Pam has mats.

Pam has hats.

Am I a sad, sad cat?

Focus Skill

 Make Predictions

You can **make predictions** about a story. Use what you learn from the story and what you know from real life.

Look at these pictures.

You can use what you see and what you know. You can predict that the girl will probably take a bite of her food.

58

Look at these pictures. Tell what might happen next. Why do you think so?

Try This!

Look at the pictures. Draw a picture to show what you think will happen next.

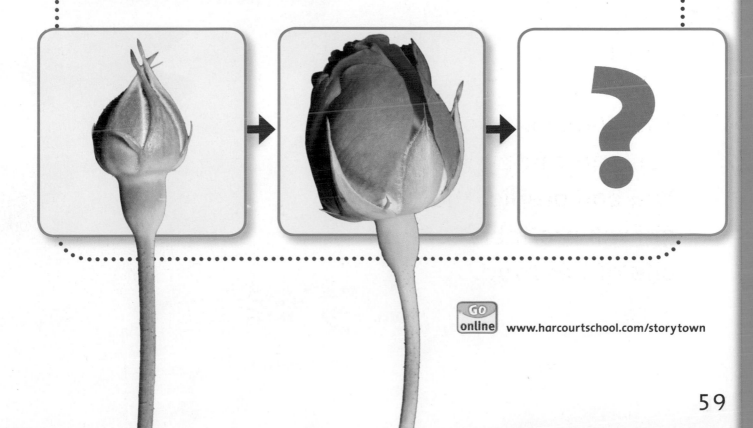

GO online www.harcourtschool.com/storytown

Words to Know

High-Frequency Words

in

too

no

I sat **in** the van.

They sat, **too**.

Can we go? **No**!

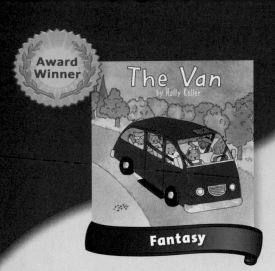

Award Winner

The Van
by Holly Keller

Fantasy

Genre Study

A **fantasy** story has parts that could never happen in real life.

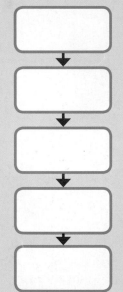

Comprehension Strategy

Ask Questions As you read, ask yourself questions. Asking questions will help you think about what you are reading.

The Van

by Holly Keller

Sam has a van.

Pam sat in the van.

Max sat, too.

Dan sat in the van.

Pat sat, too.

Can the van go?

No!

Jan can help.

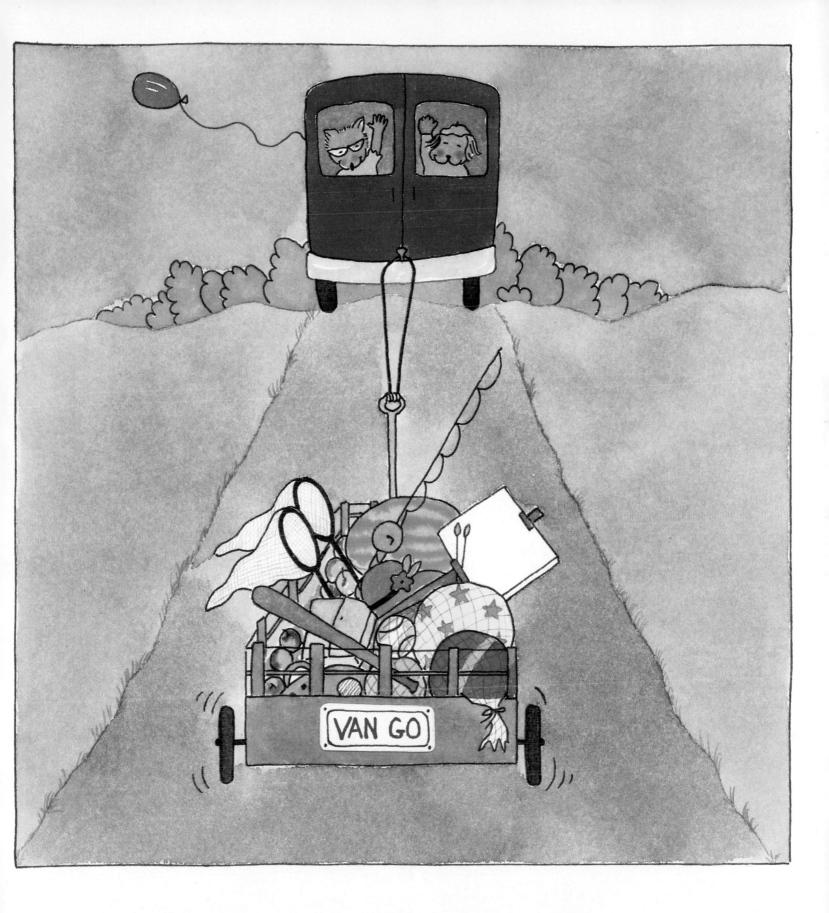

Now the van can go.

Think Critically

1. Where do you think the animals are going? Why do you think that?

    MAKE PREDICTIONS

2. What happens when Sam's friends put all their things in his van? CAUSE-EFFECT

3. Who solves the problem? How?

    PROBLEM/SOLUTION

4. Could this story really happen in real life? Why or why not? FANTASY/REALITY

5. **WRITE** Do you like this story? Write about it. WRITING RESPONSE

Meet the Author/Illustrator
Holly Keller

Holly Keller loves to draw animals doing things that people might do. She never had any pets growing up but says animals are more fun to draw. She gets her story ideas from things she did as a child and things her own children did. She says that children's lives are full of stories.

People
Movers

Nonfiction

People Movers

People move from place to place.

Sleds help us move through ice and snow.

Boats help us move through the water.

Special trucks help us move through sand and rocks.

Connections

Comparing Texts

① How would "The Van" be different if Sam had a boat from "People Movers"?

② "The Van" and "Let's Tap!" have friends helping each other. How have you helped a friend?

③ Tell about an activity that you would like to do with your friends.

Writing

In "The Van," Sam and his friends bring their favorite things with them. Think of what you would bring and why. Write about it.

I would bring my kite.
Kites are fun.

Phonics

Make and read new words.

Start with **mat**.

Change [t] to [p].

Change [m] to [n].

Change [n] to [c].

Change [p] to [t].

Fluency Practice

Read "The Van" to yourself. Then reread it with a friend. Take turns reading aloud until you can read the words correctly and easily.

Contents

Lesson 3

1 Get Started Story

Miss Jill

by Anne Mansk
photographs by Doug Dukane

2 Genre: Nonfiction

Big Rigs

by Paulette R. Novak
photographs by Doug Dukane

Trailer Truck

by Bobbi Katz
illustrated by Bob Staake

3 Genre: Poetry

Phonics
Words with short vowel i

Words to Know

Review

now

let's

Miss Jill

by Anne Mansk
photographs by
Doug Dukane

82

Miss Jill has milk.

Miss Jill sits in a rig.

The milk is in bins.

Dan will fill the rig.

Dan will fit it in.

Now kids have milk.

Let's have a big sip!

Phonics Skill

Short Vowel i

The letter **i** can stand for the sound at the beginning of **it** and in the middle of **mix**. This sound is called the short **i** sound.

Name these pictures. Each word has the short **i** sound.

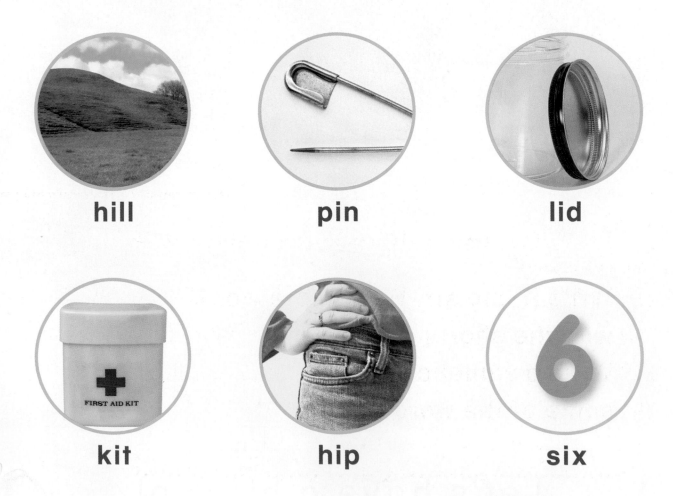

hill   pin   lid

kit   hip   six

Read each sentence. Choose the picture that goes with the sentence.

It is big.

Jill will fill it.

GO online www.harcourtschool.com/storytown

Try This!

Write **it** and **sit**. Write more words with the short **i** sound. Write a sentence with some of the words.

it
sit

Words to Know

High-Frequency Words

so

hold

get

home

soon

This is **so** big!

Look what it can **hold**!

It will **get home soon**.

 www.harcourtschool.com/storytown

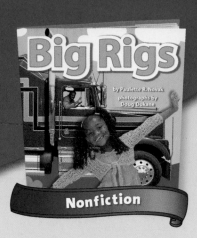

by Paulette R. Novak
photographs by
Doug Dukane

Nonfiction

Genre Study

In **nonfiction**, words and photographs can work together to give information.

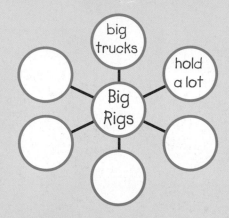

big trucks

hold a lot

Big Rigs

Comprehension Strategy

Monitor Comprehension: Make Inferences As you read, think about what you are learning and what you already know. This will help you understand what you read.

94

Big Rigs

by Paulette R. Novak
photographs
by Doug Dukane

This is my dad.

This is his big rig.

Big rigs are so big.

FIRE EXTINGUISHER INSIDE

Look at what big rigs can hold!

Dad sits in his big rig.

Fill it up!

Now Dad will go.

Get home soon, Dad.

Think Critically

1 **What is a big rig?** CLASSIFY/CATEGORIZE

2 **What do big rigs do?** MAIN IDEA

3 **Where do you think the big rig in the selection is going?** DRAW CONCLUSIONS

4 **If you could meet the people in the selection, what questions would you ask them?** PERSONAL RESPONSE

5 **WRITE** When you grow up, what job would you like? Write about it.

WRITING RESPONSE

About the Photographer
Doug Dukane

When Doug Dukane was small, he used to visit truck stops to look at all the big rigs. Now Doug is a photographer. He thinks big rigs make great photos because they are colorful and shiny. "It was fun to sit in one and take pictures for this story!" he says.

GO online www.harcourtschool.com/storytown

Trailer Truck

by Bobbi Katz
illustrated by Bob Staake

We are buddies. What a pair!
We go together everywhere.
What's a cab without a trailer?
Like a ship without a sailor!

We whiz along the interstate.
From coast to coast, we carry freight.
Oh, how wonderful it feels
to roll along on eighteen wheels!

109

Connections

Comparing Texts

1 How are the story and the poem alike? How are they different?

2 What is your favorite kind of truck? Why?

3 The cab and the trailer are buddies in the poem. Think about one of your friends. Tell what you like to do together.

Writing

Think about "Big Rigs." Make a list of things that a truck might haul from place to place. Choose one thing and write a sentence about it.

A truck can bring apples to the store.

Phonics

Make and read new words.

Start with **<u>wig</u>**.

Change **g** to **n**.

Change **w** to **t**.

Change **n** to **p**.

Change **t** to **r**.

Fluency Practice

Read "Big Rigs" aloud. Remember to look at capital letters, commas, and end marks. This will help you know how to read aloud each sentence. Make your voice sound like you are talking to someone.

Theme (2) One for All

Instrumental Zoo II, artist unknown

113

Contents

Lesson 4

1 Get Started **Story**

Pick a Sack
by Linda Barr
illustrated by
Laurence Cleyet-Merle

2 Genre: Fantasy

Get Up, Rick!

by F. Isabel Campoy
illustrated by Bernard Adnet

Cock-a-Doodle-Doo

3 Genre: Nonfiction

115

Phonics
Words with ck

Words to Know

Review

too

have

Pick a Sack

by Linda Barr

illustrated by
Laurence Cleyet-Merle

116

Nick has sacks.

Pick a sack, Jack.

Pick a sack, Mack

Jack has his sack.

Mack has his sack, too.

Jack and Mack have gifts!

Kick it, Jack and Mack!

Words to Know

High-Frequency Words

oh

late

yes

Oh, no! It is **late**!

Is he sick?

Will he get up?

Yes, he will.

GO online www.harcourtschool.com/storytown

Get Up, Rick!

by F. Isabel Campoy
illustrated by Bernard Adnet

Fantasy

Award Winner

Genre Study

A **fantasy** story has parts that could not happen in real life. In many fantasy stories, animal characters talk and act like people.

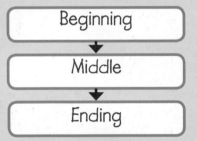

Beginning
↓
Middle
↓
Ending

Comprehension Strategy

Summarize After you read several pages of a story, stop and think about what has happened so far. Summarizing parts of a story will help you understand and remember the whole story.

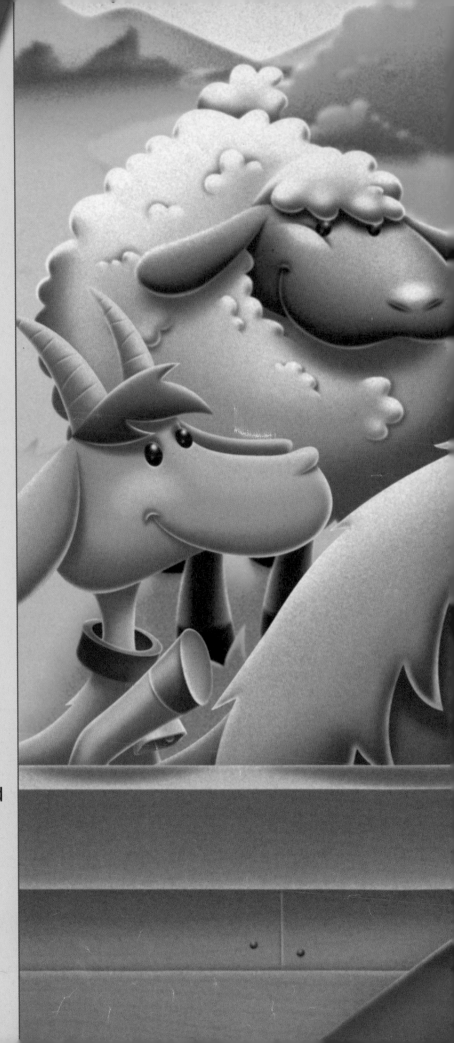

128

Get Up, Rick!

by F. Isabel Campoy

illustrated by Bernard Adnet

Oh, no! It is late!

Where is Rick?

Is Rick sick?

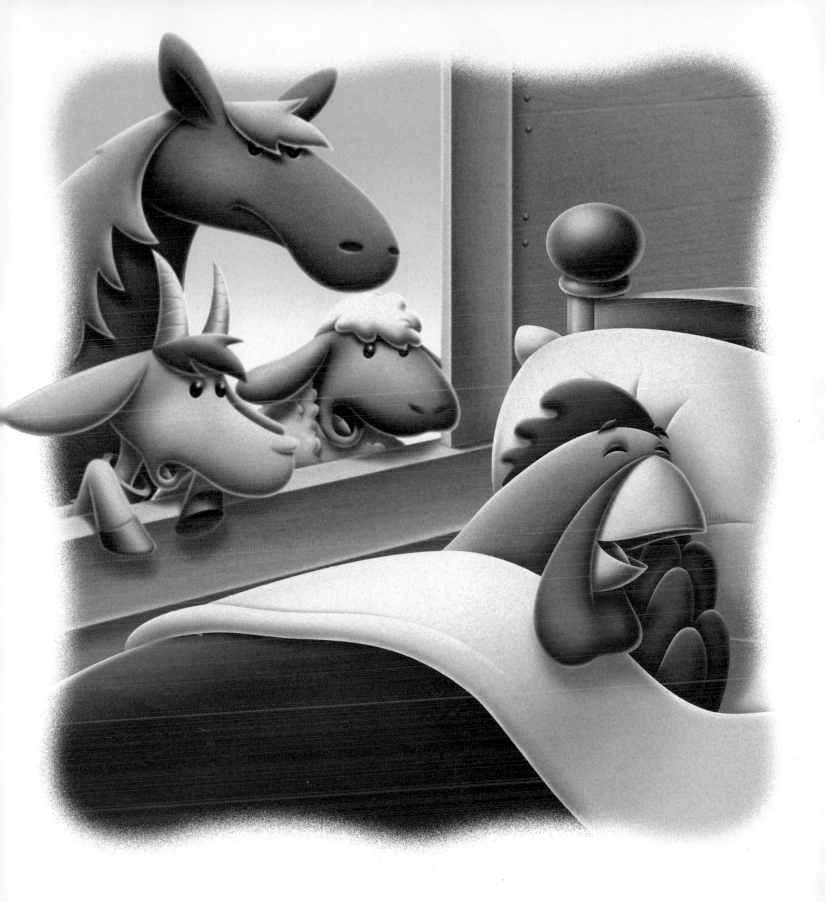

No! Rick is fast asleep!

Get up, Rick! It is late!

Cock-a-doodle-doo!

Oh, Rick, it's too late.

Now Rick is so sad.

We can help Rick.

Let's get him a gift!

What is in the sack?

Will it help Rick?

Yes, it will!

Cock-a-doodle-doo!

Think Critically

1 What happens at the beginning of the story? BEGINNING, MIDDLE, ENDING

2 How do the other animals try to help Rick solve his problem?

   BEGINNING, MIDDLE, ENDING

3 How does the story end?

   BEGINNING, MIDDLE, ENDING

4 Could this story happen in real life? Why or why not?

   REALITY/FANTASY

5 **WRITE** Which part of the story do you think is the funniest? Write about it. WRITING RESPONSE

Meet the Author
F. Isabel Campoy

F. Isabel Campoy lives on a ranch part of the year. A rooster wakes her up every morning. "He doesn't have an alarm clock either!" she says. "I wanted to imagine the opposite situation, and so I wrote about Rick."

Meet the Illustrator
Bernard Adnet

Bernard Adnet grew up in France. As a child, he spent many hours alone drawing, but he also drew for his nieces and nephews. Today he still makes children happy with his drawings.

Cock-a
-Doodle-Doo

Nonfiction

Teacher Read-Aloud

Cock-a

Roosters crow to mark their spots.

In the United States, I say, cock-a-doodle-doo.

In Japan, I say, ko-ke-kok-koh.

Contents

Lesson 5

1 Get Started Story

Jobs
by Anne Mansk
illustrated by Sachiko Yoshikawa

2 Genre: Realistic Fiction

Dot and Bob
by David McPhail

Trees Help

3 Genre: Nonfiction

Phonics
Words with short
vowel <u>o</u>

Words to Know

Review

no

help

what

do

good

Jobs

by Anne Mansk

illustrated by Sachiko Yoshikawa

Dad has a job.

Dad digs and fills pots.

Don has a job.
Don can help Dad.

Mom has a job.

Roz has no job.

Roz can not help.
What job can Roz do?

Roz got a job.
Good job, Roz!

Focus Skill

Characters

The **characters** in a story are the people or animals in that story.

Look at this picture.

The children are the characters.

160

Look at the pictures. Point out the characters you see in each one. Tell how you know they are the characters.

 Try This!

Look at these pictures. Tell which picture has characters and which does not.

Words to Know

High-Frequency Words

much

find

thank

162

Bob is my dog.

Can you **find** him?

Bob helps me so **much**.

Thank you, Bob!

GO online www.harcourtschool.com/storytown

Award Winner

Dot and Bob
by David McPhail

Realistic Fiction

Genre

A **realistic fiction** story seems like it could happen in real life, but an author creates the story.

Who	Where	What

Comprehension Strategy

Recognize Story Structure As you read, ask yourself questions. Who is the story about? Where are they? What is happening?

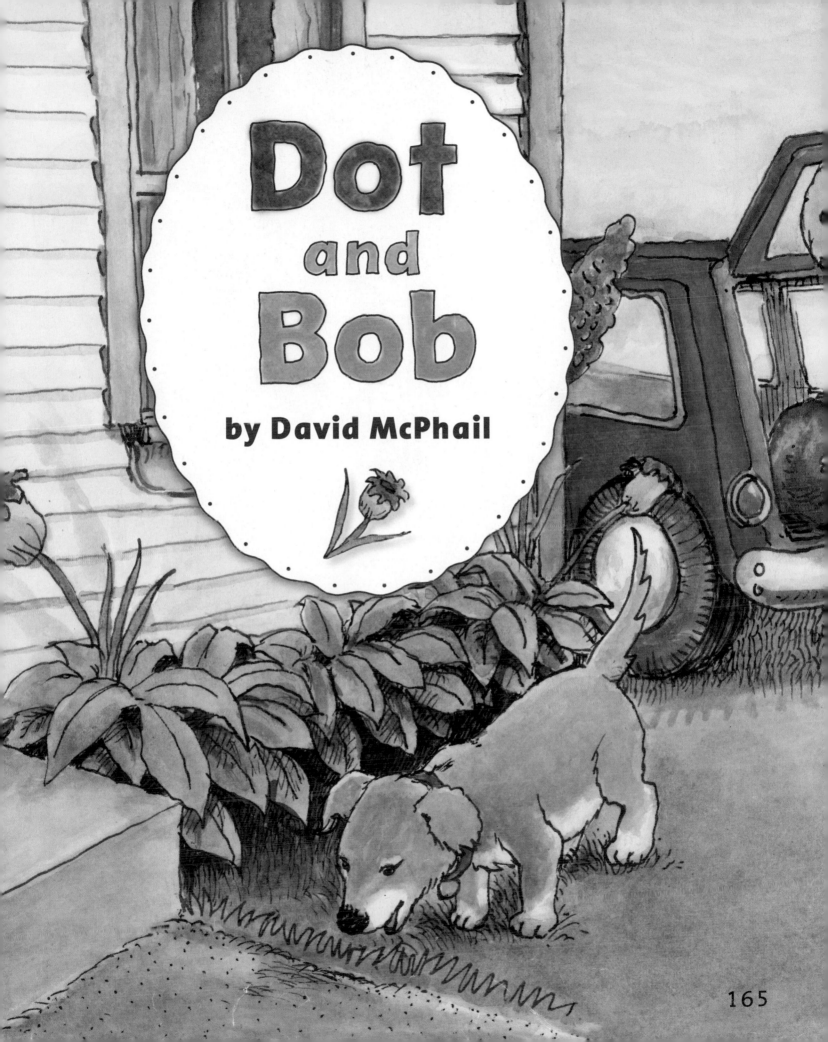

Dot
and
Bob

by David McPhail

Bob is Dot's dog.
Bob likes to dig.

Oh, Bob! Do not dig there!

Mom has a tree.
Dot will help Mom dig.

It is hot.
It is too hot to dig.

It's not too hot for Bob!

Bob likes to dig.

Bob digs down, down, down.

Did Bob dig too much?

Mom will find out.

Look at the tree top!

Bob kicks and kicks.

Now the tree fits.

Thank you, Bob!

Think Critically

1 Who is the character that helps Mom and Dot? 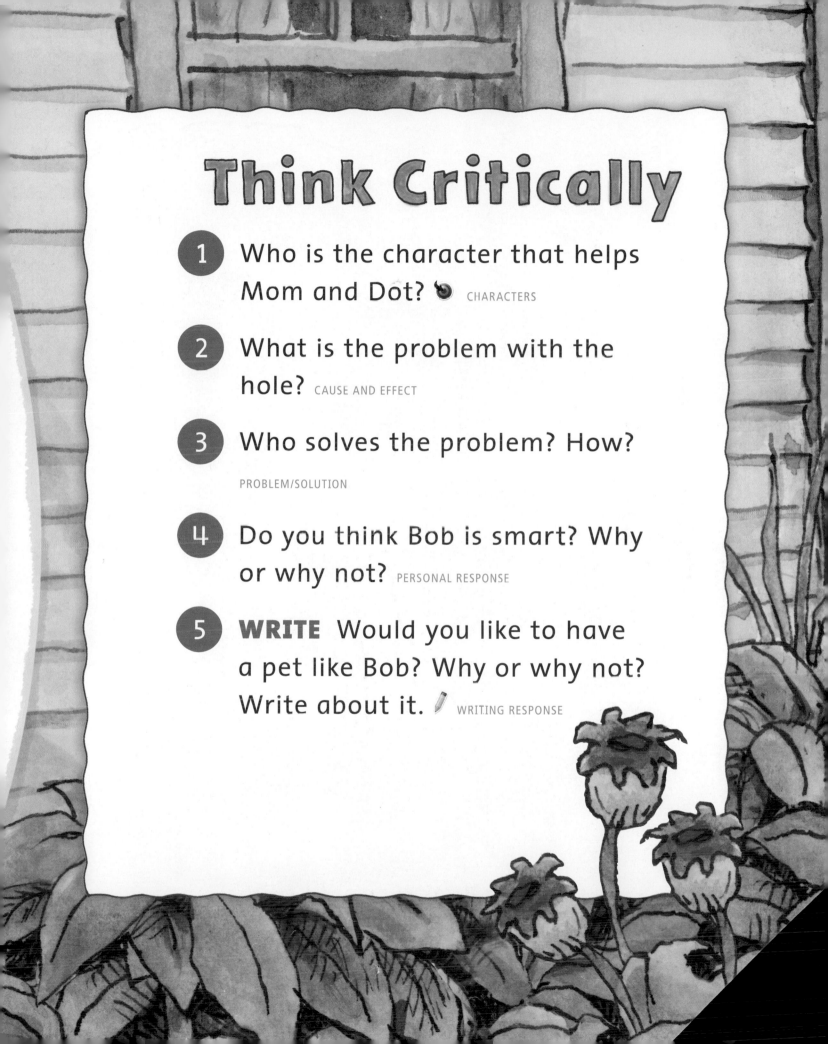 CHARACTERS

2 What is the problem with the hole? CAUSE AND EFFECT

3 Who solves the problem? How?

PROBLEM/SOLUTION

4 Do you think Bob is smart? Why or why not? PERSONAL RESPONSE

5 **WRITE** Would you like to have a pet like Bob? Why or why not? Write about it. WRITING RESPONSE

Meet the Author/Illustrator

David McPhail

David McPhail started drawing when he was only two. He would draw with a black crayon on paper bags that his grandmother cut up for him. David thought this story was fun to write and draw. "I love how the pictures help a story take shape and make sense," he says.

GO online www.harcourtschool.com/storytown

181

Trees
Help

Trees Help

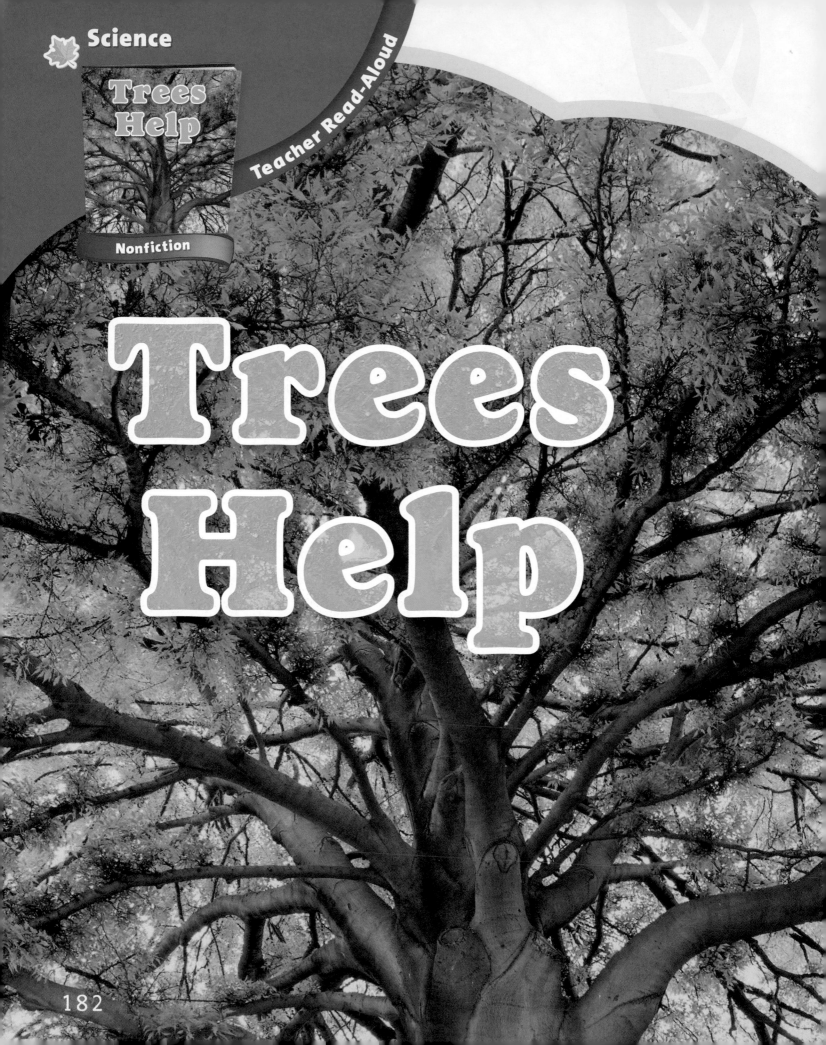

Trees help give us clean air.

Trees are homes for animals.

We use wood from trees.

We eat fruit and nuts from trees.

183

Connections

Comparing Texts

1 How are the story and the article alike? How are they different?

2 Which pictures did you like best? Why?

3 If you were going to plant a tree, what kind of tree would you plant?

Writing

Dot and her dog Bob helped plant a tree. Think about something special you and a pet might do together. Write a sentence about it.

My cat and I could have a picnic.

184

Phonics

Make and read new words.

Start with **<u>hot</u>**.

Change **h** to **p** .

Change **p** to **d** .

Change **t** to **g** .

Change **d** to **l** .

Fluency Practice

Read "Dot and Bob" with a friend. Follow along and listen to each other. Help each other read the words correctly. If you make a mistake, your friend should help you. You should help your friend in the same way.

Contents

Lesson 6

1 Get Started **Story**

A Tall, Tall Wall

by Deanne W. Kells
photographs by Steve Williams

2 Genre: Nonfiction

All on the Map

by Lucy Floyd

illustrated by Max Grover

Roads

by Elizabeth Spires
illustrated by
Sachiko Yoshikawa

3 Genre: Poetry

Phonics
Words with <u>all</u>

Words to Know

Review

where

finds

she

for

up

A Tall, Tall Wall

by Deanne W. Kells
photographs by Steve Williams

Dad has his map.
Where is the wall?

Pam finds it.
She calls Dad.

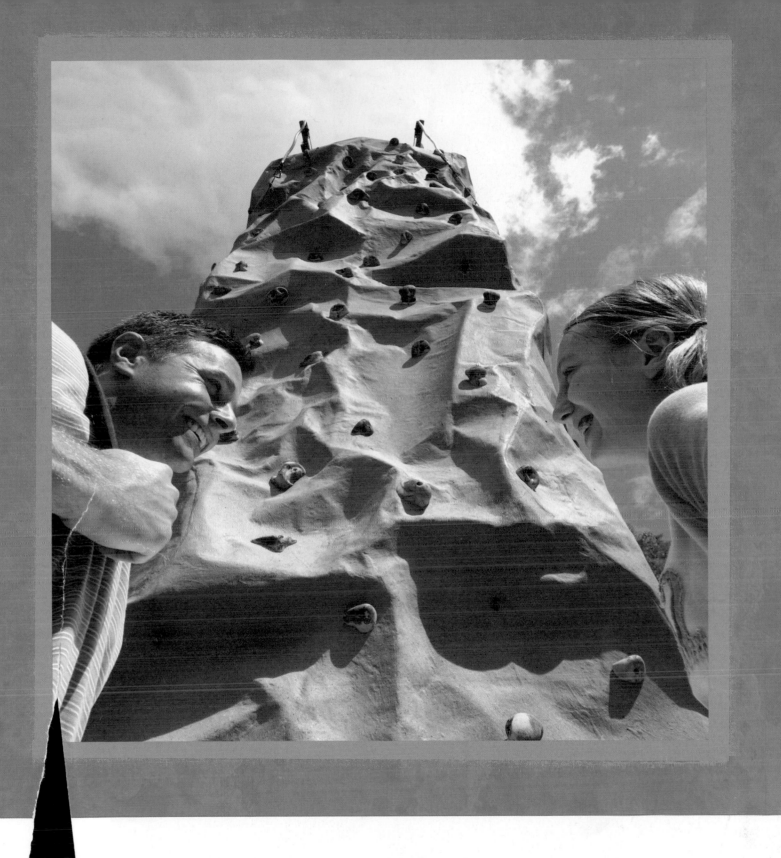

It is a tall, tall wall.
It is a rock wall.

Dad packed a lot.
It is all for Pam.

Dad has locked Pam in.
Pam will not fall!

Pam zips up the tall
rock wall.

Pam is on top!

Phonics Skill

Words with all

You have learned about spelling patterns. You can see the spelling pattern **ap** in **cap** and **map.**

Another spelling pattern is **all.** By itself, **all** is a word. Add the letter **h** to the beginning of **all** and you get another word. The new word is **hall.**

Say the picture names. Run your finger under each word. Look and listen for **all.**

ball

wall

call

Read each sentence. Choose the picture that goes with the sentence.

1. It is tall.

2. It will fall.

 www.harcourtschool.com/storytown

Try This!

Read the sentences.

This is a tall wall.

The ball is in the hall.

We all like the mall.

Words to Know

some

make

of

how

198

I see **some** hills.

I can **make** a map.

All **of** the hills are here.

Look **how** I did it!

GO online www.harcourtschool.com/storytown

by Lucy Floyd
illustrated by
Max Grover

Nonfiction

Genre Study

Nonfiction selections give information. Many nonfiction selections use photographs.

Photos	Maps

Comprehension Strategy

Monitor Comprehension: Adjust Reading Rate It is important to understand what you read. Reading more slowly may help you understand the information in a nonfiction selection.

All on the Map

by Lucy Floyd

illustrated by Max Grover

Here is a big town.

Here is a map.

Here is the town hall.

Find the hall on the map.

The town has lots of land.
It has some hills.

Can you find the hills?

Look at how tall they are!

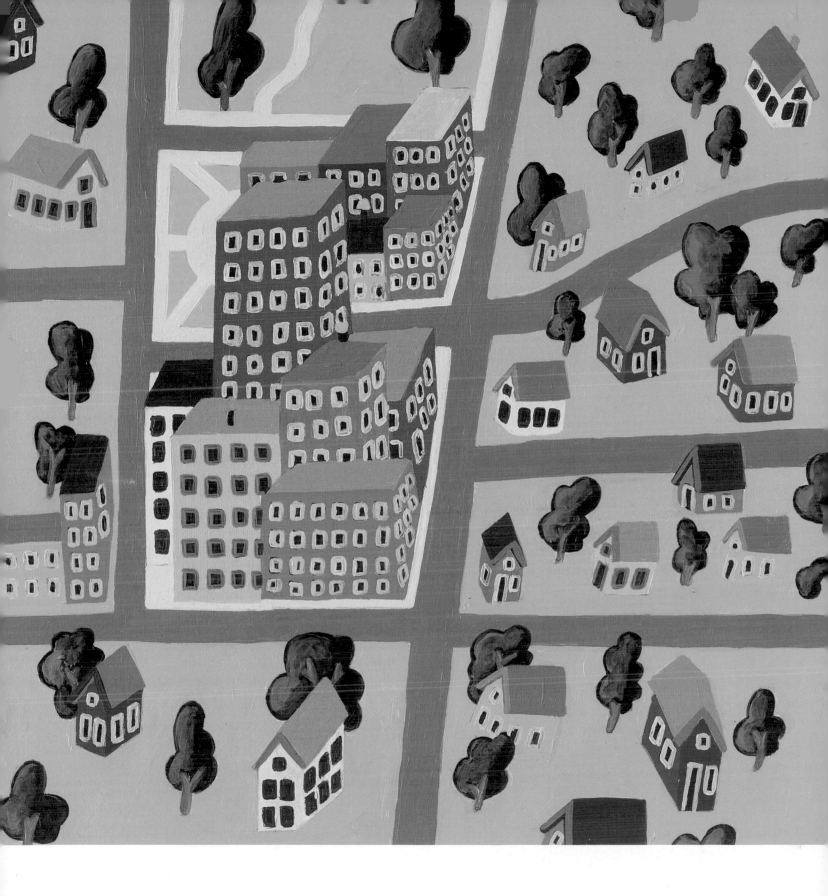

They are on the map, too.

What is this called?

It is on the map.
Can you find it?

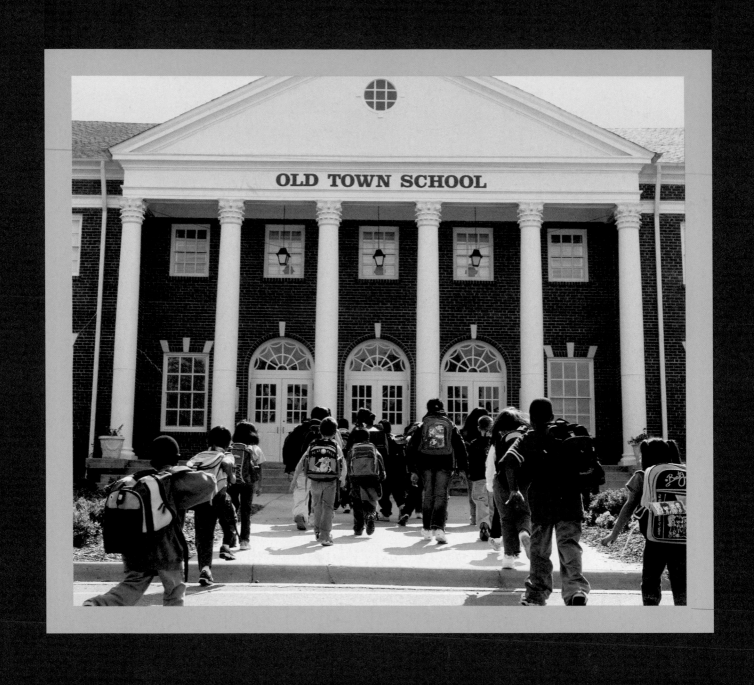

Some kids go here.
What is it?

Find it on the map.

They all like maps!
Now they will make a map.

Here it is!
You can make a map, too!

Think Critically

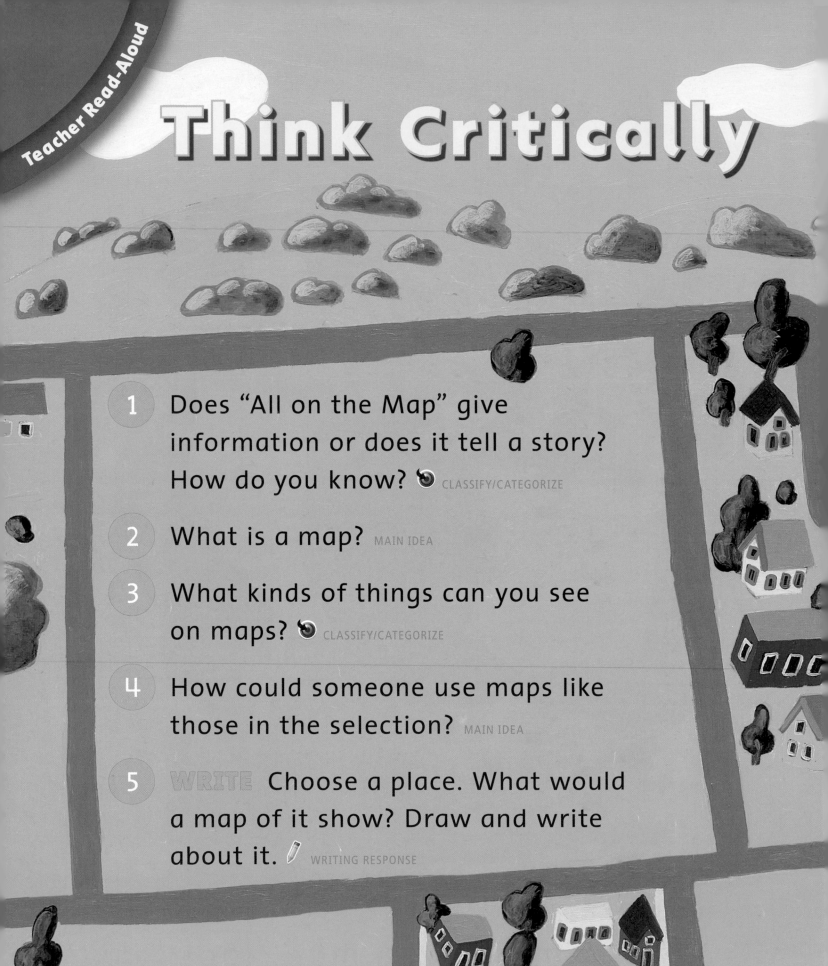

1. Does "All on the Map" give information or does it tell a story? How do you know? CLASSIFY/CATEGORIZE

2. What is a map? MAIN IDEA

3. What kinds of things can you see on maps? CLASSIFY/CATEGORIZE

4. How could someone use maps like those in the selection? MAIN IDEA

5. WRITE Choose a place. What would a map of it show? Draw and write about it. WRITING RESPONSE

Meet the Author
Lucy Floyd

Lucy Floyd has written many stories. Some are make-believe. Some are about real people doing real things. "I enjoyed writing this story," she says. "It reminded me of trips I have taken. Pictures on a map helped me find things."

Meet the Illustrator
Max Grover

Max Grover enjoys painting pictures, because he loves trying out new colors and showing the world the way he sees things. "I enjoyed illustrating this story because I love maps," he says. "I like the colors of maps and the squiggly outlines of roads."

Roads

by Elizabeth Spires
illustrated by
Sachiko Yoshikawa

Poetry

218

Roads

by Elizabeth Spires
illustrated by Sachiko Yoshikawa

North, south,
east, west,
we run along
and never rest.

Where are we going?
Everywhere!
We never stop
until we're there.

Connections

Comparing Texts

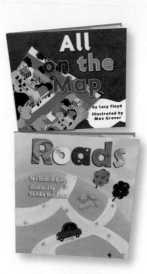

❶ How do roads and maps help us get where we are going?

❷ What do you like best about each selection? Why?

❸ Do you think big rig drivers use maps? Why do you think that?

Writing

Think about "All on the Map." Now think about places near where you live. Write a question that a visitor might ask you.

What is your favorite place to eat?

Make and read new words.

Start with **hall**.

Change **h** to **m**.

Change **m** to **t**.

Change **t** to **w**.

Take away **w**.

Fluency Practice

Read "All on the Map" with a friend. Remember that an exclamation point shows strong feeling. Help each other read the sentences with the feelings that best match the story.

Glossary

What Is a Glossary?

A glossary can help you read a word. You can

look up the word and read it in a sentence.

Each word has a picture to help you.

gift   She has a big **gift.**

dad   **Dad** can help me play.

dig   She can **dig.**

dog   The **dog** sat.

down   Pam fell **down.**

G

gift   She has a big **gift.**

H

help   Liz can **help** Ann get up.

hills   The **hills** have big rocks.

hold   I can **hold** Dad's hand.

home   This is my **home**.

hot   The pan is **hot**.

kick   I can **kick** the ball.

kids   The **kids** ran.

L

late   Oh, no! I am **late!**

M

map   This is a **map.**

no   **No**, you can not go out.

sack   This **sack** can hold a lot.

sat   Tim **sat** down.

sick   Jack is **sick.**

van   **Let's get in the van.**

Acknowledgments

For permission to reprint copyrighted material, grateful acknowledgment is made to the following sources:

HarperCollins Publishers: "Wag, Hop, Hide!" from *Good for You!* by Stephanie Calmenson, illustrated by Melissa Sweet. Text copyright © 2001 by Stephanie Calmenson; illustrations copyright © 2001 by Melissa Sweet.

Margaret K. McElderry Books, an imprint of Simon & Schuster Children's Publishing Division: Untitled poem (Retitled: "Roads") from *Riddle Road: Puzzles in Poems and Pictures* by Elizabeth Spires. Text copyright © 1999 by Elizabeth Spires.

Scholastic Inc: "Trailer Truck" from *Truck Talk* by Bobbi Katz. Text copyright © 1997 by Bobbi Katz. Published by Cartwheel Books.

Photo Credits

Placement Key: (t) top; (b) bottom; (l) left; (r) right; (c) center; (bg) background; (fg) foreground; (i) inset.

8 (inset) Digital Stock/Corbis/Harcourt Index; 24 (t) Cathy Crawford/PictureQuest; 45 Cathy Crawford/PictureQuest; 59 Scientifica/Visuals Unlimited; 76 (b) Alaska Stock Images; 77 © Ilene MacDonald / Alamy; (c) Ray Manley/SuperStock; 82 (bg) Guenter Rossenbach/zefa/Corbis; 90 (t) Robert Pernell; 90 (cl) Graham Prentice/Shutterstock; 91 (tl) Emilia Stasiak/Shutterstock; 91 (cr) Marc Dietrich/Shutterstock; 91 (c) Paige Falk/Shutterstock; 92 © Ken Davies / Masterfile; 98 (bg) Reza Estakhrian/Getty Images; 100 (bg) © Ken Davies / Masterfile; 111 (cr) Stockdisc/SuperStock; 112 (t) M.L. Campbell /SuperStock; 115 (bl) SuperStock, Inc.; 148 Uschi Hering/Shutterstock; 151 (br) Masterfile Royalty Free; 160 (c) Dynamic Graphics Group/IT Stock Free/Alamy; 161 (c) Jon Smyth/SuperStock; 161 (tr) Marvin E Newman/Photographer's Choice/Getty Images; 161 (tl) Michael Newman/PhotoEdit; 161 (tc) Photofusion Picture Library/Alamy; 161 (bc) PureStock/SuperStock; 182 (c) Brian Lawrence/SuperStock; 183 (t) Greg Probst/PictureQuest; 183 (b) Hein Van den Huevel/zefa/Corbis; 183 (cl) Ingram Publishing/SuperStock; 183 (cr) MedioImages/Getty Images; 196 (bc) plainpicture GmbH & Co. KG/Alamy; 196 (cr) Swerve/Alamy; 197 (tc) Andre Jenny/Alamy; 197 (tr) Beateworks Inc./Alamy; 197 (br) Khoo Si Lin/Shutterstock; 197 (tl) Peter Gridley/Photographer's Choice/Getty Images; 198 (t) Chris Bence; RF/Shutterstock; 201 (bg) Jim Wark/AirPhotoNA.com; 202 (c) Jim Wark/AirPhotoNA.com; 204 (c) Jeff Greenberg/PhotoEdit; 206 (c) Rudi Von Briel/PhotoEdit; 208 (c) Jim Wark/AirPhotoNA.com; 210 (c) David Young-Wolff/PhotoEdit; 212 (c) Will & Deni McIntyre/Corbis; 220 (t) Cristian Marin; RF/Shutterstock.

All other photos © Harcourt School Publishers. Harcourt photos provided by Harcourt Index, Harcourt IPR, and Harcourt Photographers: Weronica Ankarorn, Eric Camden, Doug DuKane, Ken Kinsie, April Riehm and Steve Williams.

Illustration Credits

Cover Art; Laura and Eric Ovresat, Artlab, Inc.